furnish, entrap

Kashif Sharma-Patel is a poet, writer and co-founding editor of the87press. Pamphlets include *relief I willed it* (Gong Farm, 2021), *fragments of mutability* (Earthbound, 2020) and *Suburban Finesse* (Sad Press, 2020) co-authored with Ashwani Sharma and Azad Ashim Sharma. *furnish, entrap* is their debut single-author collection. Kashif writes criticism and runs a newsletter culture hawker https://kashifsp.substack.com/

PRAISE FOR *furnish, entrap*

Kashif Sharma-Patel walks us through their urban worlds of cr0 and LDN, centres of the multiculture imbued with critical study. Come, listen closely— feel the sonorous vibrations of the impeccable and focused linguistics served up in their debut. Sharma-Patel flexes contemporary disaffection and alienation with intellectual prowess, backed by rich strategies of wordplay and dialectics, their sensibilities attuned to texture and taste in phenomena, aesthetics and meaning-making. Mythopoiesis here wraps us taut like a coarse silk, a detail that embellishes the moment and memory of play— although play here is the desire for play and desire's own play, contrastingly across thought and embodiment. A gender-queerness emerges familiar and fresh nonetheless into the open field of the page. Even while fielding, the match itself is a vehicle for play—fifty overs soundtracked by wafting sub-bass and close rhythms, accompanied by the scent of grill.

— Nat Raha, author of *of sirens, bodies and faultlines*

Kashif Sharma-Patel is tuned to gentle frequencies and the rough notation of our most exacting music. Hey, this book says, your lyric is showing, sprawling like the city and spilling like a street. It's new like the day is awake all night.

— Luke Roberts, author of *Home Radio*

Sharma-Patel's use of the tongue is a feat in itself within the pages of furnish,entrap. furnish, entrap makes lightwork of using language to stretch across space, concepts and emotions. These poems unfurl right before your eyes to unleash a battering of poetic verse of "(para)literary exegeses". The political-poetics of furnish, entrap have consequences and are a call to action once you have read them.

— Jasmine Gibson, author of *A Beauty Has Come*

An electric collection of poetry, furnish, entrap by Kashif Sharma-Patel excels in its political dissection of contemporary society, but also in its observation of the human condition and what it means to exist in a world that stretches us thin. Ricocheting between questions of sexuality, gender, diaspora, cultural inheritance, colonisation, queerness, the west, the east, and the socio- economic, it is impossible to escape the sheer turbulence jammed into every stanza. But the brilliance here comes from allowing these themes to inhabit the words, to live and breathe within its structures. In doing so, Sharma-Patel has sculpted a poetics of original beauty that inhabits with such eloquence the mind and vision of the reader. One cannot help but see things previously unable to be seen, to hold them, and in this conclusion absorb the power of this book and be forever changed by it"

— Stuart McPherson, author of *End Ceremonies*

for Narinder Sharma, my Dadi
(1934-2013)

ISBN: 978-1-916938-11-3

Cover designed by Aaron Kent

Edited and Typeset by Aaron Kent

Broken Sleep Books Ltd
Rhydwen
Talgarreg
Ceredigion
SA44 4HB

Broken Sleep Books Ltd
Fair View
St Georges Road
Cornwall
PL26 7YH

Contents

prefatory poem   9

I: SHORTS
subtended quotidian   13
double graphic pole   14
gully to gully   15
on a dismas bambai ting   16
the motion of light in water   17
Chillies   18
The house-endings   19
an audiography   20

II: SEQUENCES
culture in common   25
phantasmic folds   27
numinous verges / maidan   35
[ekphrastic motion]   37
the two genders   39
thresholds   41

III: RELIEF I WILLED IT
[PSNS]   47
inductive motility / iconicity's reprieve   48
[relief I willed it]   52
corral / recondite / a constitutional   54
[perio - surround]   57
sicilia   58
[cenobitic…]   59
city cognition   60
maqbool   61
docile in bed   62
ash is purest white   63
spelling names   64
isherwood under duress   66
cannabis by the tracks   68
[lacuna…]   69
states be   71
trump in gj   73

IV: SAFED SHAHAR

safed shahar: mutable prefabulatory remarks   77

V: DICTIONARY OF EXHAUSTED SOUND
[ABRIDGED]

bh-   93
mai-   94
mu-   95
-nath   96
cro-   100

VI: OPEN-FIELD

[open-field]   105
bam bam brilliance   106
make it/already done   108
prehistory of they-them   110
"frippery"   114
[after carpentier's los pasos perdidos]   117
accosted at 11.30am   119
Raam ke Naam   120
garba in-script   121
[agora as open-field]   123

VII: FURNISH ENTRAP

furnish coffer elemental   127
cr0 lyrical entrapments   135

Acknowledgements   141

furnish, entrap

Kashif Sharma-Patel

Broken Sleep Books

prefatory poem

the fissuring of thought,
being and institution as everyday.
the intimacy of things.
dwelling in phenomena, culture,   aesthetic   suspension,

the movement of urban, that eddying

queerness, raced existentialism,
undercommon imagination,
desedimenting desire, the push
to radical tradition,

pushing to a neurotic edge
to search the
trace, to trace the ashes,
stutter at the deconstructive

edge, back to kitschy
filmic splendour,
high modernist returns
low modernist revolts

autofictional impulse, travelled
immanence, autoethnographic
thresholds, adventurist renditions,
redolent languaged genericisms

I

subtended quotidian

head freeing — out in front
body numbed in painkillers
and exhaustion
a cocktail of distrust
time vibrates in the nook of
the bus's embrace
a public unto itself

double graphic pole

after the kid

that start and end internecine
text as life takes hold
silence and interpenetration
at the end of the book
beginning the writing
beginning the book
becomes the writing
like a double graphic pole
between desire and narrative
and social actuality
where becomings keep rolling —
in that internecine space
of writing and place

gully to gully

shard sold out and
elemental elocutions //
cosmopolitical characterisation
at the cross of Edgware Road and
Church Street as market wares
pass hand and cloth drapes
in bouts of cultural assertion
across the navel's allure

on a dismas bambai ting

the hung realist
anthology of violence
where the script reactive
ripped-up and restitute
an anglo-indian antagonism
where leadership seeps silken
and histories begun

the motion of light in water
after Samuel Delany

erratic nerval interstitial rerouting
recurring irrelevance unremembered
recalcitrance
cornucopia internal reformed and paved

ordered force of interaction pillared by a
material desire where process fails to meet
place, where falange remain salient,
irredeemable–revoking narrative

social wiring–homosocial
(para)literary exegeses
where the Indian meets southern judgement
at the cusp of blood's legibility

> *In turn the place extends as structure*
> *replaces movement, or movement*
> *resists being reinstated*

Chillies

St. George's Circus

Train up
turning corners following
perception — decision-making
as meaning-making

grotty river walks and rampart-
like ascents, wet and untrustworthy

colombian-inflected bus-rides and thigh-high boots
giving glances in terminal movements —
roads as arterial shards pumping artillery

~

corner restaurant glistening / *filmi* music and
husky men at work in that lateness
of the familial -
chicken curry pilau rice and a silver pot
filled with masala tea -
milky hot and sweet
cup-and-saucer interminable as
ageing men work crosswords and boys
jostle for a drink and a bite

Colding walk and
a scramble for charger
dishevelled and fresh

The house-endings

The ending of farce / the social
an uncoming and nervous passings
and non-happenings like distant thuds
crashing down interior walls slowly
and interminably like a distant remembrance
a coming to the tongue, bitter and distasteful
and quite unheard of and really unnecessary
like why aren't people normal and understanding
and so misreading our situation so often and why
do I have to assert because in asserting something
is lost, a choreography and interiority is sullied
and homogenised and made rotten when/if
reality is only understood as transparent
and forceful and wholly put-together
as if one's situations was stable and not
unfolding in distant hysterical manners of
uncertainty, mundanity and some incredulity.

Money's paid and I give up.
On to the next hunt.

Freedom for the social, the non-space and imprecise and
unstable and opaque dislocations of feeling imparted
through sentiment and regimentation — through and against genre —
developing practice I do hope in incremental revolutions

an audiography: [club, dub, dancehall, front room, giddha, playback]

I

big sugar's crooning a voice
    /into presence

at the tip of lkj's finger
    /on the railton road

like the last doyen of hustler's skank
    /at the edge of culture's wit

a re-embodied detournement
    /of the showcase
    /a fledgling script
    /a dirty scrap
    /a disappointing derivation
    /crisp

II

dreaming voices down phone
cut and clear on their sofas
in the hubbub of domestic or
the whirring of the outdoor
vapour recollections of the night
thereafter where character grates
and the social is set-down

III

aaj kaal   remnants as
　　　　elders reminisce

images   re-hearsed
　　　　in the wake of loss

careful　　　　　in　　-　　　scripture

audiographic　　　　　fealty
　　　　the first utterances

enmeshed with tongue
　　　　punjabi yesterdays

folk's tales in the suburban excess
　　　　historical redress

II

culture in common

uncle clifford in sway and sound / authorial
extant, feeling self through vision / southern
gothics and sensual practices / [grown and
sexy] land disputes, rentiers on our mind,
space for anxiety, rancorous realty / looking
for aesthetic utopia in dialectical antagonism /
courtly space, woozy and offbeat / kharms
and mayakovsky / asiatic stuckedness,
traditional desedimentation meaning all that
is held in mudra dispersed / the sovereign
steppe a membrane of dislocated desire / the
filmic ouvertures of khamraev and gulya /
we wrote & drank coffee wrangling
subjectification, antagonising over faustian
deals and proliferative programmes,
awnings of arterial rushes / body
channelling the concurrent vistas of social
immediacy in rat–a–tat largesse. I ate split
pea, pea shoot and fried leek in ciabatta and
mapped the city through gay promise and
portentous mystifications / the sea beneath
the street — sewer and calc, hard water and
harder spite / laboured and lost / down river
and drift / pick up TV and rest / the subject
morphs on / O essay O mournful copy O
cream O broken guile / halt this vessel for
poet needs disembark / the motor functions

wrong, our direction not mine / I bid
farewell and descend layers in Miltonic
distress / culture in common, find transit
through here / Times Square Purple London
City the Deuce at Wimbledon spectacle /
find me a house and a muvva / give me
strength of reply and remonstrate cybernetic
grievances dressed up in social machination
/ the end of headache crumbling counterfeits
and commodified linguistics / fake as
cheese, chips for all

phantasmic folds
after Mackey

I

vampiric longing the sweat and smelt imperious, irascible
/ the jauntiness of malkovich directing plays / kinski
corrugations, ferrara's walken, / the rats rise up, blood
spills in gothic materiality / the contagion lustfully
accepted / pre____ slashed / chronicles in the louisiana
swamp / _____ erotic longs, parisian guilt, the grandeur /
of pomp and sensibility / a campness incalculable in the
hands of unctuous accelerants /a slowed down-ness / the
history of aching / movement (the polaric twist and
foundational / fullness, brimful and cellular compressing
device, rerouted for gravitational translucences /
monotheistic assurity a step gone, turn back into the
hinterland and find the people, grammarian paralysis, the
phoneme is drifting along interwoven with mythopoetic
urgency / the force of the gods / clairvoyance as plot-
points, genericism as comforting irony, while the
cybernetic undergrowth moves subject to subject against
the barrage of p2p flagellation / opinion dissipates as we
re-scend / as ascension into the world, at the end of the
self, seeing the world, in the gulf of transcripted
abstractions, we tricked / the entanglement a pure
transfixion of sensual matter, an auto-fictive eroticism
where body meets metastised retort / the transglyphic
lingual cut an impure strain on the weathering of time, a
darkening of space, alveoli, the phantasmic folds of
durational pressure, a choreographic reverberation

submerged in fracticality / our transcendence a eurasian fatuousness / dialectical permutations perambulate our desire to mediate self — world / entropic occurrence as regaling trepidation aggrandising for a future draconian in its relevance

II

send them to coventry
>disappearing switch-blade
>control —
making sounds on paper
turbanned virality
we living dead
the juncture
ending load
the giraffe's breath
>lathe turned out
as if iridescent reality punctured
>illusory realism
we saw earth acclimating
wizarding tomes to a dying light
the curled up hair reverberating the
>sensuous versioning
we found viable visionaries on the
>lanes of turbanned abodes
carrying returns to soils off-world
>off-site contracting the rivulets of
>a dying speech, multiple scripts and
>still we lie in indolence

If revolutionary breath weighs on the mind like the soul-sucking vampiric, then sensation dwells in the contrapuntal penetrations, excreting reactive fluid in the wettened visage of Arjuna's repose

The cut of Mirabai's lyric a bhajan further than I /
farther than the mind's eye and psychedelic
pomposity a vacated lingual-space, peopled in
variance, reciprocation provinations we people the
planet under whip of pathogenic virality; the contract
non-sensual at the end of the Raam-Lila where
Ravana's head slight twist in a curling moustache for
the mythopoetic acolytes drive through contagious
revenations

III

We never liked the crass interjective revulsion
cloaked in interest / fetish for a poor boy / our song an
I to behold at cross of river bend onto pastoral
wayabouts, argot auratic in taut risque, weren't
mustered in blended mood, more lyrical excess for
the interpenetrative paroxysm, never-before here-nor-
there heard-not-seen the eyes betray while elephants
forget the tuneful clairvoyance a proselytising salve
for the balm of escapist prurience

Meaning too much

IV

nosferatu at edge of world / being /
doing /
         recognise the relevant cuts
document reminisce the time new lows
in arkham city popping off in
Jai's whip finger pointing waves aslosh
in the maritime forward / ongoing
viral load, concurrent retaliating
restitutions we were still hammering
at the sword, capacious in
tongue tied reprehensibility / no time
like free time, freed up / forces
discombobulating the retired ganja,
blood-smoked reverb wash in the
darkened boiler room where extraction
finds new victims / abstraction the
pull away in isotropic fealty,
interest made too broad the generalist
always loses, which means living,
winning a spate of cynical tweets
for the self employed

the floating bass at loose ends
         parse the bubbly
we're on course for pineal
         curtailment
the dub at the lips opening, oldie
         pilgrimage and knowledge
we practise on in webs of foreboding

reality / cultural sanctioning for

the profane a sight held too far

flee indivisibly

formed spite splicing ventricles unaccounted

for on road,   re-wound

par-took, a drink,   through nook

and crook, handing over mic for the

PA kept under wraps, too high in

the mix, keep it subdued, locked under.

V

lighted up we transferred

down Bhaju's line of direction,

vectors of faith weren't nothing like

palpable tawdriness / curdling force,

leaning in hearing / irreverent

sparsity at the end of the firework

bang — riddim feels like this

numinous verges / maidan

pressure like disoriented strange energy / idiolect /
quaintrelle in training / desiring synthesis but more /
much more /

indwelling ludic bloom
mystic sweetness , sweet
beast , numinous verges

gollum   exoskeleton
my brain a mediating technology the market foggy
and resplendent , aura of arrival, forgiving misstep /
mistake / hateful associations / the word comes
better / more / rays burst in overdetermined
retrospectives where revisionism mere sleight of
tone / inquisitorial voyages for wolf eye all mangled
words turned virtual web, soothsaying for birds
tailing off / generous offerings for the dogon mystic
/ the lightness of mind turn spirit in the everyday
prakrit / lyrical excess / overflowing cirri of urban
walk / the multiple offerings from craft
contemporary, ethnic scatterings, a conceptual
impress - ment swollen over with sambal, coffee
sriracha and vanilla custard / bärlauch and spaghetti
all'assassina / the acid brimming where time — shift
warps in teleportal junctures and sexually torn
vistas / at end of mogo chip, rhizomatic lingerings /
we built up an artifice shred through with biotic
dexterity / a cyber-rehashing, ungovernable mass

organised along precepts already attuned, vital and
victual / look for third man, find trans-fem avatar

multiply–seen, many seeings

central parks, crepusculent wholes

move together, jagged redrawn

harry hotspur and compressed repairs

[ekphrastic motion]

———

ekphrastic motion
that golden shimmer
in city farm allure
a rewind auratic
retention
in keeled knots
surface the indigent
a hanging parameter
revealed tactile
stained glass rays
in multi-formal
conviviality

_____fury
writing walls cut
down voice
cleared out faculty
fanciful forwardness
an imperial stance
senseless obdurate
set a   -   light

———————

city mourning

        gender cut   embodied

        tongue wrapped

        mongrel assimilation

progressively becoming

counteractive   —   collapsing

we spoke in quick time

double step

deep routes

felt body licked

hidden in taste

the two genders
on mangoes and watermelons

at the turn movement
too fast where undergirdings
switch locals affronted
as magazine shoots innocuous
glances in icy conditions
conditioning rays at the
corner of virtuous assembly
colonial marking in attire
subgenre dis-attachment
reverberates as legibility
         cleans

shards of overground warmth
in midsts of atmospheric assault
furtive retreats into rhythms
foreknowing first
mangoes of the season
the originary tale of the cultivar
golden and alphonso judgements
crude shouts besmirching badamis
swelled noses and men in skull caps
wheeling juicy tales
compelling myths of origin
a kind of bare veniality

outpouring at another rotation
axial limits in guarded
contrapuntal melody

where the rain comes   operation
voice regales, recounts,
earnest and weighty
continentality right

multiple dis-triangulations in
laughter
non-fluous
sweet surprises
in swift succinct strokes
at tip of watermelon knife
layering dreams past done

thresholds

after mahmoud darwish and bülent ersoy

I

invisible visible

the making before birth

as threshold of identity

absent in its point

bodily transaction

presented in prehistoric

                        violence

along the stretch of contemporary

                              freedoms

voice transferred for bleeding

                           Presents

II

if halfcut at axis when trauma turn left and coaches stand at oper-
ations in check, istanbul futures on bridging scars where wounds
cauterise at the half-axial movement, modesty's mistress mistrust
interpellative action ready-made already done in-action / daily
humdrum urban milieu, sunflower pips, spread of salad, chorba and
cacik, chai sipped in ancient action from saucer to lip, traumatic
recurrences papered over with lino / rock psych and western garb
/ neo-europe as post-asia / polyglot returned as de-transitioned
exchange / goods revealed orally, pre-auratic stance wrapped in
plastic, paper-bag running cherry-tasting / vegan summoning in
venture entrepreneurial ethno-business as linen-stripes and faulty
light-switches / permeable archipelagic ardour as parabola pasts
intersect at disjunctive points — cultural, epistemic, performative
— turkic presents, london town fecundity in social breakdown —
waking deaths — unmarked problems, urban problems — passive
polities, politically rife, resolute insolence, antagonistic elevations
— unsuccessful navigations in colony collapses, culinary condi-
tions for ripening palates / aesthetic form distributed inordinate
and detached / detailed debasements laundered in high-rise shores
/ widening paths occidentosis in post-islamicate tomfoolery /
verlust at the hole-in-the-wall post-prole pre-capitalist perfidy /
performed resignations / i breathe confessional warmth / i eat in
essence / in pre-common state / i wish to bodily frame / through
the blessed queers / the pre-lingual affectation, the movement of
lingual judgement and nominative justice / the face of an-other /
one an-other / browning health / sub-porous intent / an ethical
recognition / the canteen as relation / the disinterested hospitality
as being brought into the fold / choice done away with / bedecked
in throes of wonder, guilt, fomo, restlessness looking to us here in
content gliding possibility

/   after the event vibes

III

in wakening softening cherry skins,
taut (socratic) growing burdens of speech imposition —
outed inferences in the growing toil —
i was speaking rhetorically —
the conversation kept on non-verbal —
communication continue —
tanning slowly under kitsch suites —
dulling desires, caught in two —
over leisure in multiple desires tanning
consumerist in a bid for connection —
destructuring reminisces as post-nostalgic /
the conversing in absence after *absence* /
a further coming down /
evading a figures placed bodily straight and strict /
machine gun coloured administration in the head
weighing down like the original subalterns /
twisted queer lives — multivalent — street smart *girl* /
 weathered woman, service male, petit flaneur,
casualised poet, pre-fabulatory gusto and angst

III: relief I willed it

we were para-sympathetic as
          sun drizzled light

and goldfinches call   *contact*

          breathe in
                    out

cycles aspirating gnawing

cawing

inductive motility / iconicity's reprieve

avatar
avatharam
the descent into being — being ...

    being ... gone
    bereft of that hard stuff
    whetted underfoot, perfectly
    capable / adaptable
the philological constraint / lost
    unfound when willed it
the hubbub no longer interested,
a drink for a lively one,
    repeat the conditions,
    shed light

        feeling desperate underpass
        under the — pass — touch
        that — anybody — not here
        the neon signs shuttering release
        the posture erring slantwards
        the hubris of things, the red chilli
        unearths through the spinal column
        energy flowing trickled thenceways
        not-ever surfacing slow inductive
        sonic allioles resembling iterative frailties
        the development legality furnishing

generate the mythopoetic intimacy where
        nandi tells us shiva lies
        with the undergrowth
the folk matkas in hand oil dripping
        as steam filters through
        digital space, the vernacular frame
quickly coloured in the dirt in
        the construction struck overseas
the building site locating
        coordinates of truth — being
truth — yourself — as channeled
        flux, variant pillory, clumsily
billowing, public shame

                the long march in burnham beeches
                top of slough, tales of hockey
                and semi-profi genealogies,
                skill trumped by clinical euro-
                astroturf, the linguistic cut a
                pollarded axiomatic

    we sang and breathed and
    wished anew / *filmi* music,
    faux categorisation
    we lived against category,
        perennially behind, uncertain,
        returnable
    we laughed, cajoled, bantered, survived,
        speculated, seriously and irreverently
    we systemised our wonder, losing words
        elsewhere, the marking's

signified our coming-together,
our failure at category, our
instituted failure to do —

we instructing ourselves of the finer
points of failed categories lost
patience with the auxiliary and
archaic boffins of individuated
society

we tried to find a language for our
              weirdness and inconsistency,
              occasionally landing on something
              substantive, often laying in wait,
              wayward and bereft
we tried to position worth as tangible to
              feeling, overwhelming forms of value
              with bursting sentiment and
              counter-rational jibes, joviality
              abundant in the cooling autumn
              breeze
we loved each other, got annoyed, lost
              our orientation, performed
              rituals against intention and left in
rushes of white light in the

saccharine
              utopic

understood resistance as a conducive thing
kept on move, words doing their thing

phoolan devi
more time
people doing things
the dial doesn't work
thugee time
jewel in the crown
fantastic utterance
my practice more time

on

tone

iterations of hope

looking like that end of
time   —   done   ;
          relative
to the conduct aetiological
            phalange
          curve left
anacrusis curtails commit ment
            striations revel
          circuitous rapport
was ra '   approchement
          in the songs of 'raah'

[relief I willed it]

relief   I willed it

bobbing and basted

insouciant scions

cloying

rill

modicum

*

hold line
straight line
om upright
    -ness
red - lite
lightness
overviews
archeophonic
    occasions
at the syncopated
    tracing out of frame
in concrete textual heresy
    as material in motion
    suffers under weight

of dread, colour, face
kabir's face, an outlining of
    temporal duress and
    aesthetic release
forge across, the folks
    still speak

manipulate the headedness
wax lyrical in the wake
    lyrical difference
    a hybrid cause
    we talked and talked
    it was a nothing

*

michael imperioli tells us
don't you just love these long
rainy afternoons in new orleans
where an hour isn't just an hour
but a little piece of eternity dropped
into your hands

murky knees
and bad light stops
    play
looking for models
    reconfigurative terrains
    for a renewed purpose
    at the end of an
    architectonic

corral / recondite / a constitutional

corral   reprieve

tomahawk   gestures

bear   grease   slick

tales loyal and laconic

métis   —   the historical juncture
                                    dwelling
                                    dealing
                                    compelling

*

in distance   indis - tinct

                     the verge / regress

                     eloping openness

i mean when the despair got callous, too much — like turned inward / joyless banging / dance parties r lonesome, loathsome / the jaunt of arm re[a]ffirming, gaunt of the telephonic camaraderie in articulate to pangs of besottedness / facetious doing / knowing the outcome, wanting to interject while knowing the outcome, but staying presumable, provisional, provenance adhered-to while internally admitted [?] adjunct, one forgets possible assuages, the external dis — alienating effects of action sought for, recombined, redolent, ultimately relenting in its everydayness like running supplies in the siege, palanquin at the ready in the hidden jungles for the great juggernaut / men with scone, butter, bread, jam, eggs, bacon, coffee, cup, knife exuding the sort of arrogance that ties repression with insolent fuckery, torpid tensions / peaceful skin / hoarding bedsheets, possible today, probable lay in lustre

and like shivering with too many words, too many poets,
written, classifiers and calculators / unsettled jungles, jobless,
purposeless, left long ago, we could think royally |—| mortally,
scraping, scrimping, sinking / looking to the perfect south-facing
bay window, top floor, dark wood furnishings, *'cheap not retro'*,
work on music, thinking, writing, travel too, stories, fabulating
times made affable, right in returning / if still, premonitions
of unsettlement, re-actioning disruption you might call it |—|
not sure if entitled to settlement, settling, maybe just *being* in
place, worthwhile, aimless, pertinent on time scales [recondite]
belied deference, longer than apricity accounted for, continued
effacement, suppressing sation, circumspect 'round the whole
accords / it weren't even like the words witnessed the duende that
was tuning the voice / it was an ethnolinguistic trait, tractus, the
framing all wrong, insert in measures, material perspicacities |—|

[perio - surround]

perio - surround
stereo aground

post punk modernism
wandering mystic
fragment — constituent
an expanded sense of personhood
i presumed i auto-graphical corollary

promontory
secula

it's about possibility and potentiality, like doing a really good
book review, like how to outline and stretch thinking and peo-
ple–socially, generally, linguistically–like as specific subjects, in
idiomatic accentation, broader cultural icons–iconicity or virtuos-
ity–like something emanates into the writing–not really poetry,
or poetics really–more like sense, or sensibility, maybe mood–but
its not like cognitive or even sensory as such, nor that affect-lark,
more visceral and vital, maybe scattered & epic both bound

sicilia

straub & huillet, 1999

orange chased me

        down

            the

        street

my words became

      subject to —

origins to —

failing to —

the bare bread n valley life

      asperity in frame

anaphoric postulation

[cenobitic...]

cenobitic

                              anaphora

                              epistrophe   symploce

vaudeville

                  city heard

teewee

        character life

happenings

an inchoate, play of reference

heavy onset — set a path anew —

            recalibrate ? redefine ? the berlin

                  years, but in glasgow?

                  still in bowie's rapport

                  of patina and luck

city cognition

after joseph jarman

overtones + subharmonics

mad?
dad city / siti / sitty /
    like advancement
    like the sound — words
    made entails
        trails
        toiling forth
        brick no mortar
        regale with repurpose
the avium - perambalur pulse
        push off
        mis - use
the hell of where we are ...
            revisioning ...

maqbool

bhardwaj, 2003

the genre as capable / chaste /
[it continues]
 blurred sartorial gesture
 garbed minor epics for a city
   fable of much report
 we mapped the city and we found
   san andreas / the heart centre
   as open-field, soft visions of
   imitative delimitation
 the melodrama as brechtian
   strat / desultory

cultural work, journeymen in
 the molten swell of postpunk
 finest

docile in bed

bed nah read too much wired init
verbs + words floating in half awake
awnings, rakish — accruements
of transactional fictions — troughs
of dualing genuflection — greasy
chicken hands, pelau [*sic*] and barfi [*sicker*] on
the dravidian corner, a fetish for the
ones about form

20 years fresh from desh through
peripatetic decisioning, virus in the
brain / membrane / you know / that song /
the way it used to be / nah? /
the ways things used to be /
the strangeness / silences 4'33 /
radical possibility / in the kaufhaus
place

telluride, compounding adjunct-cy

ash is purest white

zhangke, 2018

second world staining

underground shirting

righteous corruption

discreet punctures

taut thighs

(tech)

coal price slumps

turkic displacement

great reformations

drunken speeches

miners revolt

dancing on the ends

leather trenchcoat in volcano shadow

spelling names

senseless, affectless
'you do and I think it's right';
sharp to shame
clarity muddied
push pencil paper
not notified
autofictional terms
                    torpor
waves wash
            ain't enough
            freedom of the fruit
            luminous brush
            through tendrils bushy,
            from pillar & post
            imitating life
            life / mates / madrigal
it was time for affectation
            the frame, wonder's wander
            motional, seasonal, ground
                    — level, further listless
            burn-bridge ?
felt finger's map setting out
                    with little gumption in
            throat
preternatural moorings
            I am constraint
                    constrained

the glorious outpourings of
                    untrammeled
          socio-cultural saturated mix

          pure style — vogue — sonic
          excellence, inhabit space, place
          and smoky tones of liberation,
          moving contemporaries — 'we',
          without agenda, pure bookishness,
          nights of passage
                    subcultural awnings
                    panning, inchoate apertures,
                    mail inert, sunken desire
                    as writerly repository, induced
                    wordliness, image — making,
                    syntactical dictional nous
                              (flow)

isherwood under duress

auden took isherwood
shiva saraswati
  shades of being strewn
  out in blue light
the rambling hills of open-world
  drive clean
I aint
look new narrative
ultimate possibility
tendrils |—| exorbitant
utterly so |—|
the page paper nah it werent off
 — said
 — say
keel, even, balance, off
nonverbal irreverbable / irreversible
 elongating
 elongue — ating
fabio dusting off groove down
24/7 vocal fries, warble, waft
we all go down if we stay together
  Rashad right
blend that shit in
 we out here
 electro steppers
 fission news
 listless fam

petulant facetious

dreaming old narratives

shaka like

under duress like

cannabis by the tracks
English, August

scene set by dakshin roadside

idli sambar swimming

tea saucer

night halts

tagore in the sheets

sex in the temples

national roads, wells

naxal trouble

people thinking

cutting nose

to spite petty

roar of delhi-calcutta

through scent and tiffin box

tongue-wrapped queues   *life*

anglo-indian troubles

development stock — gandhian goods

the dhaba bustle, kerosene and chhole

[lacuna...]

lacuna aporia impinged anabasis parabasis
catachresis - creole conceit

> *metathetical prosody trochaic cadent*
> *metric shape punctuated*
> *inflexion unyielding*

beckett quadrant

performance
sonicity
angular reverberations
soft
suspending judgement
affecting familiarity
donning / jackals
freedom of |—| from |—| comic
character
the indelible drive of artistic culture vs
            industrial desire
industrious desire
pace animated
phenomenological accumens
in furlough
arte / ars / kunst / verein

the theatrical as option / open — out
            feel taut [aught]
            impassioned

i mean it never really about all that nah not really more a little
prosodic practice / keep the brain swelling in neuro-typical
denudations / the cultural the most militated / maleficent perhaps
but neva too much / ctch tht sun / fk govt / frz veranda-ring news
philandering cues / aetiological reprisals take root corrugating
relic mainstays / it wasn't fathom as much as the hype gridded
at deadlock's passing grin / the open-air returns febrile neurality
pass cloth thru broke doors / jack it up

sometimes you lose yourself in the city
like a loss needed
where the spilling out
touches you

dis-alienation is finding pythons in west london and
                marmoset monkeys in north

the storm left doors closed
slick wet cobbles

"all full of flats"
all full of flats
all full of flats

states be

after nisha / the night before

take photo   darker rooms

imitable   geeze

spring   clean

taste the day

take the day

oyster rich / *reich*

easter rich

turn the page

take the purge

        page

cut back

kanth   /   cant

granth /   sahib

divine - city - writing unpunished

dharmic levelling

homosocial tentatives

      muscled over, unleavened

      lexicographical carriers into

         impure per–chances

incongruous gender sheen

in abstruse alveolar

    ridges

linga, sadhana

orthopraxical gestures / mudras

      burning chilli out the throat

      brown bellies belying full consciousness

      Marxist-Maoist-Ambedkarite Thought fractional

warping sexual anodyne fantasies

      the weave of worlding

      formal coupling

            (copulation)

            cognation

            corresponding

                  contingency

~~metaphysic followed philosophic?~~

non-semantic ritual soundings

exhausted meanings /dare to dream-ings

trump in gj

car honking through W1
crystallising tomes
heavy onset over dosas and bhelpuri
we wandered thru under passages   annexes
petulant to time and incredulous
the floors   piped   infra -   structures
petulant to time and incredulous
grey-pantone backdrops luminous
and lucky, level four, samosa boxes
and yellow match-ups
we slid in ruts and reeled jovial
red hot news

ached weakness, indifference, rhetoric
filial moseying, prurient in the degree
absurd dissipation

IV: safed shahar

safed shahar: mutable prefabulatory remarks

I want to write something longer, more tender,
greater space, maybe marginalia, some travel, kinda
autofictional, but also weighted and light. Peter
Gizzi talked on an online stream of his poetry as
auto-graphical, that is: he's writing his life, not *about*
his life. This isn't even necessarily a conceit, not pure
solipsism one would hope, more like a grounding
topology of reading, thinking, breathing, what
emanation

Like the constraint of form, and autodidactic release,
reaching reticently for agreeable consumption.

We used to build shit, they said on the docks; *we
used to know shit*, none of this grandstanding, right?
Probably not, but anyway we were looking for
sweetness and light, vortexes that sucked up spare
and unending time — rent — expectation.

autotelic

somatics groundedness the edges of racial
technologies where queers and browns rally, amidst
mediocrity, though mediocrity's a ground worth
fighting for, right? The ultimate test. I looked in self-
representation and saw oat milk and agave syrup,
the pustules less granulated than reverberations

unduly expose their unearthly fulcrums. The word-
play a wanting to like, like a wanting to write, that
inadvertently interpellated as machine-grinder
cognitive-mapping underling — trapped in a
web of family, affect, impotence and the ever-so-
occasional outburst of righteousness and delivery.
Delivery here an important cycle of retribution
bestowed and undertaken on behalf of underlying
protestant persuasions, southern affectations made
legible through logical rites of faux-mysticism, or
should we say the theological origins of political
will — political time. Or to break out of baseness,
a failure to express communication-breakdown —
stress as a failure to truth & sentiment. The undying
love and justice of soul music swept up, while the
mundanity and corniness of the gothic undertone
of english life makes real self-hood in detainment
and worthiness. In any case the musical innovation
for a communal apathetic experience that invites an
inner turmoil of energy and feeling holds a filmic
timeliness that mediocrity's redemption fails to hold
dear and proper. Or in failing, one feels both FOMO
for the world and for oneself. Instead application
of the recurrents of feeling and flirtation drift into
a commodifiable mode, driven into traps of labour-
inducive cognition, a subaltern trap.

*

The diaspora confessional: a problem of subjectivity.

I streamed out in lockdown and felt something. It wasn't prose or poetry, neither really film nor image, more a theoretical retelling of what hapticality would be [...] I mean the plot doesn't hold together, but its been built up to be so profound to break the artifice seems so crass and presumptuous.

The disused phone-booth at the end of the road outside the corner-shop fell over, sticking out concrete and steel. Causing a ruckus. Came back some days later to see they'd recemented it in, rather than just scrapping the old thing. Is this an archival fetish in the streets?

*

Sean Bonney somewhere - late Coltrane - indic mood - the bebop *shrill*
[...]
Alice Coltrane's more overt eastern promises — even in its scarcity; that's the promise of constraint.

Thinking cultural consumption as weaponisation

       cultural experience / haptic viewing?
       participation, contours of popular form,
       serials, kitchen sinks, visual residuality

  stories / fables / breaking lost time,
  against leisure, against irony

Still into silence, staying home, ontime, offroad, streetslinging, sunkissed, mealymouthed, cash grovelling daily exercise, glutton for prurience and artistic collaboration, the journeymen.

mango hunt like an intense recon effort, *Metal Gear Solid*-style, judgement, tracking, adaptation, sampling, travel, trace, passable stalls, origins determining worthiness, tolerability when unknowns known, deployment of critical faculty ending in satiating tales of golden wholesomeness, like a whole meditatory set-up — a technology — rolled into urban resourcefulness.

House of Hunger Marachera docco: thinking about ground-down intellectualism, colonial education, linguistic warping — not quite new articulation, not quite creole/pidgin — more like overly accented?

Anyway, is cultural consumption during social media pure voyeurism? Or a more anabased form of gossip as collective action — somewhere between clout, attitude and desire for contact, to be touched, but scared to admit, which we call adulthood, a forthrightness as a tapping / turning into frequencies and languages — again not wholly creole, maybe a spectral presence co-constituted, slang variability, vernacular spectrality.

Keep looking for restitution, promising relief,
retaliation poses, moments of clarity pared down
well in the cloudy edges of

Sweetness and light that Arnoldian twist of fateful
cliffs of yonder, whitening shrifts of gestalt and
ground.

unacknowledged and overmythologised

we need a mythopoetics of the present, against
presentism and the present state of things

real time / months in days / years in weeks / the
allusion of freedom and adventure untethered from
work and leisure / deconsecrated in eddying burst
/ felt jubilant, joyous, riotous, promises of racing
tomorrow / classy, sexy / we got rid of politics,
left with vigour anew / low level zine, lowkey
detournements from status quo, a culture war for an
end to this world

worlds splendour

manner in which grand theory can affect, guide
action/work and feedback into the genres, heritages
and
action/work/performance. The performer-artist-
spiritualist grounded, in play

Harmony: it's this thing, the imploding moment of
my virus addled brain, the set down tumbles and
fast clap cats of lowrent vestibules; the vestiges
of vestibular prosody, the imploding excerpt
from poetic time, nation time, not daily grind.
An externalised quotidian, deconsecrated, made
natural, depathologised, remythologised as a
material account of social relations — relay in
mythopoetic duress. Communism amongst the
anarchists — *blood ah go run.* Your ideological
qualms quake in temporal fixity. Fix Your
Subjectivity. Your rhizomes need tending to. Your
undecidability is the trigger for a circlusive re-
enactment; more re-adaption, an iterative process of
historical restraint, inverted deployment restoring
your thumb's integrity. We found modernism in
the streets and became aesthetes, politics on the
record became abolitionists, joy in the flesh and
were always gender nonconformists; somatic
dissidence we centred fission; formality derives,
paraontological prosaics. The audible made agonised
Trapped within shell of Bonney's soothsaying,
ripping out scabs of buried repressions, temporal
seizures; lived time, a speech-act away, yet voice so
often eludes...

Spontaneity is this latent thing that gets caught up
under your eyelids when you try to sleep. it's this
thing that keeps a tic in the back of your throat when

you try to keep working hours for work, it's this
inertia-setting thing that sees through the artifice
and you're too tired to think anymore.

*

       fragmented visuality
desire - follow that thing behind the guilt
the cognitive train keeps the brain abuzz, night.
So gather your alms. Train's a-coming. Jump off.
In the circumspectral penumbra of retaliating
more-ishness, the brevity's not for nothing. Fen-
like annexation, the red pill was a con, and the
timber rotten-through. You wrote to be gang, a
motley crew, you wrote in the face of constant
subjectivation, and your shame slipped off. You
worked for celebration, and grassy remorse. Your
parasomniac episodes shedding light on a nostalgia
for the present. You picked up fragmented, and
thought 'machines'. You picked up style, knowing
the body is a gesture away from sublation. You
repeated and repeated finding solace and ground in
the ritual of art-making.

hölderlin
prosodic faultlines, tectonic retaliations, lockdown
blues reverberating negations of synaptic pasts,
repressed edges shown in disbelief and dismal
fervour. Protect the statue, the state of things,
stay still, a surface of impropriety, dis-embodied
response to thinking / feeling — repress the

freedom drive in temporal depoliticisation and
carceral neurotypicality — alienation as the longue
duree sets in and the talking heads reassemble
for the death cult of policy making, management
and border control. Control the border of desire
and justice doled out in a stinking 24hr court;
crude and conniving; making rhythm a trap;
writerly moments not reduced to archival dust and
'expertise'. Generosity and collective subjection
vestibulares against antagonism, TV schedules; the
hardcore continuum, failing at normative genre and
trappings deranged sense over the scars of mutilated
possibility

'said being determines content, content deranges
form etc.'

the brown mutability, interchangeability as a
'creoling' of sense, not enough in prefiguring a

                              *

jamalian lightness
a happenstance of harmelorhymopoetic phrasal
globalism melismatic interpersonality

scrolling to dull the mind's eye.
wellness as productivity indicator.
calves exuding tetchy anxiety as a somatic
    response to authority.
i don't like it.

mediocrity, being out of time,
    evading the visual, vidual,
    anti individual, but feigning
    baudelairean excess and vestry
my brain collapses in ludicrous calls to
    attention and
    shameful bouts of inertia.
We tore ourselves up to remain undisciplined,
    we were torn up to become disciplined.
We evaded the social as control,
    we've invented the social as escape
We made projects, and then disavowed them
    in juvenile distaste for completion.
We wrote CVs and kidded our self-rejections,
    while chasing steady paychecks and
    community-standing, momentary
    rests.
We believed our self-hoods and then
    remembered its a crock of capitalist
    shit.
We thought we were disenchanted,
    until we needed the next
    paycheck
We tried to work it out, in art, but
    that too a petri dish for capitalist
    drudgery and false promises.
We took to the street, it was momentous,
    fragmented, and hardwork.
We were dysphoric, and hated it
    here.
We were guilty and shamed.

We wanted ignorance and righteousness.
We wanted some fiction to believe in,
   but it was all too callous and calculated.

Behind all that, the fallacy, breaking
   of fixity, being, meaning, instead
   provisional justices and positions,
gender orientation and poetic acuities

cowardice and mediocrity as
value theory

*

personal trouble
life trouble
capitalist time
family / associations

trappings
doing nothing
i want to do nothing
   change everything
   live adventure
   write mediocrely
live better
in close proximity
   to myself

my time is being eaten up
   by the forces that be

again
procrastination is being overwhelmed

lisa robertson

acephalic   clandestine
sullen, slow
sub — standard — servience
mawkishness, struggle towards
    sex and paintings

peplum,
bombast, waxingly
sartorial vocabulary
monadic locationless
citational status

'the knock-off was a document and I
was its historiographer'

proprioceptive grammar
gestural etiquette
becoming city, grid
lapellian desires
gnomic and lapidary
insouciant skepticism
clothier purloined
out of hock
calmants tersely
selvedges mitred
chrysalis armoire punctum

rhythm / time / form / passage

abstruse

*

prudence and contrition
censured relief

understood resistance as a conducive thing
kept on move, words doing their thing

      phoolan devi
      more time
      people doing things
      the dial doesn't work
      thugee time
      jewel in the crown
      fantastic utterance
      my practice more time

                    on

                       tone

iterations of hope

                      Prynne's metals

stone   weight   presence
substance   stone   power
displacement   hinterland
  overbalance of intent

aureole   poutine
  gnomon
maxim   neuro stories
                   neue geschichte
volute   phoneme.

dendrite   sylphs

  bane   spurring

   roseate   mercator

  expostulatory

  Anscultate

  dehiscent

metic

cante jondo

sluices

V: dictionary of exhausted sound [abridged]

bh–

bhajan	bh*a*-jan <u>bh</u>aajan
baj*aa*n	bhajaan
ba<u>dz</u>an	ba*j*an
bajan	bayj*aa*n
bhaijaan	bhai-jaan
bajri	bhaji
bayram	long-arm
long-tooth	full-arm
too-tall	
ful-crum	
beast-ly	beast-lich
bhindi	bamieh
mogo	bammy
bam bam	
go off	
bass-off	
bass blood	
boil off	
blood tings	
brew like	
look like	
layer up	
we talk	
beat back	
breakbeat	
pulling off	
trailing back	
and the beat goes stop	
streak off	
strike out	

mai–

maidan	mai-daan
maiden	may-daan
maedchen	
maida	mildew
azaad	maidan
azaad	zindabad

central square   cricketing shot

weekes and worrall

wickets and lattices

mayday	maydie
hospital	dance hall
figured	out
never	seen
burst	through
piss	poor
folk	lore
fizzing	for
angle	land
mata	ji
euro	ting

sterlingprynne

bastard	beer
brazen	seer

philosophes and spiky dreams ,

frozen sods and battered cod

licking curve , mustard seed

sputter off and cog recede

mu–

mughal	mongol
mughlai	mogul
business	cuisine
timur	khan
chagatai	khanate
mangal	mashhad
mossad	maula
mufti	makhani
maulvi	malkit

–*nath*

bluff and bluster
        in constructed ambiguity
mottled knots crushed
receding

                        lurk-like

juggernath
        jagganath
jagg — nath
                nath
        krishnath
  vishnath   bul-nath
meganath
        meghalayan
                doodnath
aeronauth
        nauthical
                nauntical
        lag-a-nath

        ravganath
                mogul - nath
        dacoit - nath
                    thugee-nath
                thug-nath
        tuffie-nath

                    terre-nauth
        real talk
                maula-nath
        street nath
                        world lord
                rast lat
                        meal time
        relic yard

gully tagore
caught up
curled in
jacket / beard / hair
eye shadowing
extramural
young pretender

butter down

alley sharps

recordite slide

enjambed bliss

garmi gwarn

tactile-thai

working normal

baldry ice creams

diminished whey

train rides glisten

awkward knees

put-together rides

three bridges mystery

turns hearty

order order ooorder
arder arder arde
odder odder odder
adder adder older
ahder ahder ahda

cro-

Croydon	Croy-don
Croydein	Crog-dene
Crog-denu	Crai-din
Croin-dene	

that mournful state
sorry place
guillotine   sog-seen
more   resin
slough come bombs
of Betjeman
you sod
training through valley
and will
encroaching sub-urbs
rural idyll

> finding growth in the brutal
> under bricks and concrete
> sand and sparrow

sempiternal wonder
magnificent tempers
the old moulding temporals
the sagging deposed seculars
saffron shaded presages
come friendly bombs and fall on Croydon

human folk at end of London town
edge of cricketing green, Surrey homestead
think-that
ministerium your gruesome friend

VI: open-field

open-field

                  infernal

        rivulets, external

              filigree

                      turn'd out

telluric lavishment

        memoried activiousness

                    selected

        invidious mal-occluded

fermented hymns

        martial pissant

                menial

maliement

maleficence

        paltry prorogation

                phobic mendacity

your lyric is showing

bam bam brilliance

rinse   in   out

          recoil

                                                        reverb

feel   –   between kaffir leaves

and alkaline promises

masc presents   –   *bam bam*
                                                            brilliance

                                                        seized   /

                                                        doubling visions

                                        detoxing   integral

                'pre -   sexual'

                post   -   doing

                                                        multiple visions

                                                        sovereign frailties

panto / the news at 10

political waffle *this week*

flashes of film

functional

working with desire / that thing on the tip of the brain keeping
things running, lingering

cultural history doesn't tell base — *femme*

social reproduction – that keeps going

moments with filled in gaps

hard times // pink nighties

hard to look in face of —

make it/already done

paralytic subject exhuming browned face, elegant
and intolerable. The sound of words, difficult and
deferent. I looked down the loch, past dark woods,
seismic caves, gleaming surf, ' there's a queue   '
[the mineral gulf]   gallimaufry   [sic]
  pedantic, duration, release
  superfluous larynx, foregoable and irritant
     spent down mountain
    neurotic packaging
     south-facing menagerie
       entrusted in far-out per-chance

  programmatic [new words for summation]
    my rhotic [aerotic] languor, sleeping and turbulent
     dream, we inflate coupledom
  sense particularity, sudetendeutsch, and '79 escapes
    sporadic meaning, the last stretch, the last
      breaths, make it/already done, kebab mahal,
    glasgow plans, speak against voice,
      spiel and spore, arepa con queso vegano
    der kater, the mortified past, a film in repose
      developing sense and time at crux of
    sound-warp / play / the ambient effulgence

material formation, shudder autobiographical conceit,
  ekphrastic waste, spring's fatuous beams halcyon
    moorings, coarse but copper wire, kazakh crypto,

nur-sultan, blue yonder, chechen heavies, kavkaz
fags, *category* phalanx, hardy semblance
of cathartic elegance suspended in   motion
that thought a lyrical touch   away, the
sanctified pur-view, organic time kept —
read wrong, inordinate false more bobby
fisher sergeant yobbo commonplace ¬¬¬
up the hill, chips n gravy, down pub way
west indian cricket club, tickle fancy, imitable
lot

fragrantly done the generalised kerfuffle

prehistory of they-them

I

bowie blizzard
xmas in the sun
the boozing savant
a cheeky geeze
nictitating, adventitious
reluctant, reverberate
in awkward quatrain
the spanish swill, the
german stodge
anglo dreams
indo summers
nod of head, we move on
thicc and spicy
the gyalis, hum along
in path of least resistance
showing up the social self
cocks adjacent
bon viveur, joie de vivre
my soho elegance lost in
neon dirge and chicken wrappers,
a curse on your volk,
on up the river, the
regal authority, on behalf
of footballing sovereign we met
and thanked, the spark
for sardonic bonding and humourful

technik, age of fash-pilled edginess
restraint regulated, hum
tuneful and forgiving
piece together the wrinkled convivance
rebel yell, the angsty abnegation
preying on graved mind
los sueños abrogated for
tawdry peonisation
brownian motion, blinkered and
caustic, cathartic in alter—
conceptual bathetic shrills
sharp tongues, sharper wits, sharpest
lame. The unnerving wrest

II

carnivales in soho
enclosed ground swallowed
under castilian slurs and
resonant defenestrative summation.
the somnolent creative enlistment
a corrosive wound, built blunt and
deracinated — denigrate and uproot
the tears of la furia, the durable
mester, loquacious and mendacious —
the filigree in repose abstracted condition
for a desublimated desirous orifice the
erotic swell of cartouche — delicate
tuile demanding inalienable force.
Products, involuble mass inexorable mass
malcontent melisma in the cardinal re-dress,
numismatic spurge, elude the panellist's ire
rene depestre shot through with rheumatic incession
one suspects declination, an inordinate fungibility
at hand of god's delinquent, a transsexual
screed redolent with subdulous prismatic
       recollections
banyan peregrination feeding social-politic
a descended self hood replete with conjured
transfixion and bellicose rabble-rousing.
reveal thyself dormant

III

sexological negligee   irritant
my body starts to grow,   pot-bellied and
insubordinate, a depressed heaviness planted
tethers with mordant barbs, bust-like
redolency. Scream, prehistory of they-them
as body-doubling; a time loop riddled with
maleficent betrothements. Erogenous mitigation
the idiolect rebuts lateral drift; a chuntering
film, a veracious sybaritic, counterposed
with the slovenly settledness, tremulous
prevarications, larvae in-script.

> ailments, pheromones
> penetrate, ulcerate

"frippery"

I

internal slice solar

terrific larynx the excrescent

nodule pilf'ring paternity

the petrified forest, samadhi glooms

inveterate mulishness, maladroit function

the kentish ale, beast, rule-breaking

in-statutory infringement, a disinvestment of attention

tawdry discourse, subordinate presencing

a doubling primer through the gate,

straight-bat defence, mercurial wingers

chafing discordancy, reproducing conditionality

intemperate journeys, firmament against the sun,

sluicing harmonious your fripperous lot.

my money's conversational, cost-principle

pincering furnace, glottal rent

make it / your oesophageal clot

, magisterial layabout

II

difficulty in-excess
labyrinthine repositories

down walworth road, a misshapen
ode to the paralytic liquidator

moorings, another passes, numerous
modes on hand, an intensity

the mind mitigates
heady floes, the spring exhaust

longing, peppery flash, irritable —
chiliastic interregnums / an integument

of vacillating time-discipline, an irascible
blandishments, your circumlocutory famishment

a sundried particular in
prorogued suturation / maladies

at verving surrealism, swilling tumescent
decisioning, a calumny of scourging desiderata

flog this, arterial munificence
pageantry at the ready, yours, hunching

III

finish it, largessing legumes

      using, meaning, eye spilling

summer laugh, inter/se electives

      abstruse learning / hope to get along

firming it accumulative

      positivist arrestee, box em up

the build unwieldy / a fumigated whole

      plenum sacrificial, inelegant passing

          labouring dominion, yours, paratactic dialectician

[after carpentier's los pasos perdidos]

I

primaeval light
think tessellate
ground adumbrating
with kapplemeisterns aria
the soil shimmer, searching
up-river, uncovered, the garb
of modernity, a languid foil
a debasement at root of metempsychic
swelling, the lawful metamorphic
quality a gaping whole of tawdry
tendention and elusive frivolity,
aching lust in the body-in-movement
for the lustrous pagoda
penetrating perfidy, prosaic accentation
bequeathed with lustre, abashed rectitude
starched lineants, figured verlust

II

staring carpentier in the face
marxist film theory & Carlos' visage
face the bureaucratic corrupt
the assault and insult
blockade propaganda the publicity
win red and severo's escape
the moving subject at the tip of fidel's cigar
the boycott test, black and blue honours
yorkshire running red, el barrio chino,
flick through marriott's *duppies*   the trickster hiding
                                                  in spine

accosted at 11.30am

a caulked retaliation, I was tormented by petit
bourgeois north london — curbside appeal — the
heinous buffoonery, made communist aspersion
apparent — owing oligarchical ruination, but
not the Brits — natural moat, you see.
The whole thing dead time, amenable to ashen
graves, pineal expulsion you irritating twit.

The ties belong in kinetic relation; the
quantum unknowability positioned as a scrupulous
attunement of the everyman; a collation of details
morose and sleep-worthy. The commoning of
sub-social material, outgrowth of subsumed
affectation — the lyrical trace of the misstep —
written through with abstruse civility. The mores
a postulated aft a-shame; measurable dips - dish
— forgettable easings.

Raam ke Naam
Patwardhan, 1991

rollick, along, a roaming impasse,
cadge a drink. Quickly. Irritant.
Window passing, a shill, babur redolent,
relinquished moiety; a violent delineation
cut across with wrought draught —
drawing quiescence — a costive remonstrance
— a flickering of motile finitudes;
your arbitrary tracery a modulated
awning. Irking out ties unbound,
Jaya Śrī Rāma — the malevolent mawkishness
— opportune aberrations.

Smoked out florality
Peevish aurality
The lavish odious particular a
comestible delight, undergirded with
succour and tallow-like blithe

garba in-script

religious doldrum
overexpectant returns
re-evaluative returns
durational faculty
rejubilant surrogacy
sanctity

the re   -   turbulent

field   in   monotonous

entrapments   sat tightly

in   confidence satiated

spilling circles of parse   -   ness

bedouin errings
        in the slur of spring whip wind
        half step contained walks
        in fragranced contrast
        the half brothers and parish
        families cut across cloth
        halfspoken toilet ushers
        in bellicose floors
        misapprehending alignments

creaking breezy words flying for the postexpectant
gratuitous slumberers where worldly irritants pale in
pusillanimous chuntering ushering in futures implicit

plumstead motion sickness semi detached marquees patio
premature mike leigh suburban dreams — veg biriyani / chips
at morley's / momos at kailash / vine tomatoes on the go /
himalayan abodes — blessings in oil down axioms / separative
foods / in shredded chicken and salt beef and sweet breadfruit /
local honey to whom / outercity journeys with manosankar

[agora as open-field]

expunged   along   halls
     the agora as open field
         social-field, in weave
           and verb
of plangent agon   execrescent prosody
that hoyden beatitude, wistful   —   worthy
     resonant in stokey, mitteleuropa on the mind
suffusing auratic surface,   an emanation in the field
     along cracked earth / abney park's fungi
managed ruination, abundant verdure
     we succumbed to the community delight, periphrastic
amble as bodily rhythm remonstrates with
     conditioned obverse —   a history of the voice
succumbed to an aporetic supposition   dually done;
     artificial lilt as the lame leg beckons forthwith
my lyrical self aplomb with a discordant pudency
     inhabiting difficult as urchins hawk safer
bets.
          spatial fix / ground swelling with debased
     liquidity and pose leveraged folly, will it
       so. I don't think it be, a doubling carnival
     fulfilling facades of structure, tightly coiled
       phenomena.
            alight yourself duly.

VII: furnish entrap

furnish coffer elemental

I

pandemic / mass / infrastructures
need to write as mind travels,
wildly, let flow ring through
and structure appear. no need to
overdetermine or oversaturate, just
work out prose-problems and get
into the issue via culinary — infrastructural
— urban — schematic — sensorial —
contemplative — searching — gradations
— transformative — aesthetic — social
and so on
              — orthographic perhaps but none

II

coming down cricket memorings
i thought you over, whites in eyes
mind, my business
scorpion — frog
jeering calves, crunching standing
strutting channelling
calibrating the saj
foreshadowing guulit
calling out for ribaldry
mordant tones
conscious returns
lick my meshed belly and
neck adorn / verily melilla
masterful modulation
pertaining promise
in middle shroom, joint round black
wafting secrets and promise
militate against the proclaimed,
our white wine spritzer a salve for
your admonishment
felicitate and sit pretty, perilous
and thermal, the fit good and tight

III

I ate vegan cookie dough and found / street life wanting, the
compressed / striations a gaping viscera under dermis / [Heiliges
Römisches Reich] the mottled mass / facile belfry, bhelpuri
and / aloo tikki in east bustle, / golden afternoon on queen's
meadows / and kurdish meats mitigating social force / — furnish
coffer elemental / carefree, locate organ and blur through, /
ventriculated thromboid, gelatinous / rhododendron, vacillating
suzerainty / in prelinguistic angst, / the dissonant machinations
a-whir with / peregrination and obfuscatory respectability,
/ the sediments of wembley, a curse on all, / eat ruminate
retaliate the / inverted arcades, a project bloodless / on fire,
lauding compositional finesse, / a social poetic reupholstery
remonstrating / in floods, flittering levies, fursty and / free —
teufel dreich zeuge maladroit

IV

english culture in the rave out the garden
pints on the terrace chips down the street

gathering, assembly
public squares, loiter, linger,
non-abstract space
market space than a fast-paced
        commercial premises that
        dominates london's streets
sensory

V

axe to free

trunk fillip

schlanklinien

matjes

al-tiflisi

shahmaat

countenance

steering grace

tisane treat

trifling legume

concordet

being waited upon

as reorientation

control as active duality

dual power

compress terms

annotational terminance

wazwaan bergig lineants

romance and yseult

boheme street rebel

junglist judiciousness

lyrical reanimation

the blood on carpet

grid and scape

generate textual

terminate cilia

VI

sculpted like tony benn's face
crackling under foot of in-it-to-win-it
volk-dem / interrogative refusals /
agile walks slumping into rolled ankles
where CHO meets his fate and the few
dacoits triangulate the nation's timelines

talk around the said, jittery knowledge
write my tomes — rip the working class
— rip the oligarchs and colonial settlements
— rip Our Death — rip shaman's map
rip juridical speech — rip the
black sicilian — rip stick and
poke — rip the autodidact polymath —
rip the writerly eye — rip ossified
speech — rip rainy fascism island —
rip postcolonial melancholy — rip
the last whites of bradford —
rip the black greek — rip your
hauntological miscreations, we're in
the dog house, and the exit's behind u

VII

tommy tuchel

weltanschauung

against baroque decadence

kante goat

james' pocket, sterling wanting

Rudi body rudi bodied

blue on carriage

autoglass chested

dirty flags and cr0 boxpark

porto square and sanitised buses

kidding trophy the roman

descends, settling capital

debasements

living impurely in communion, the ethical

sociality / necessary poison

they all hate us we don't care

fatal flaw / passion and ELAD disposses /

shell companies and philanthropic despotism

as world watches blue down the king's

road, post-casuals meet post-soviet

geld, headhunters gone corporate,

and the body swells and twitches

to the beat of suggs

green man congregation and

homosocial organisation

the boys sing

oil and butter chicken infiltrating

my dreams

sheekh kebab and ethical disjunctures

and the people festered in festoons

of mediated zeal

bacchanal   orgiastic

VIII

eschews, desert + pint at TGIs
giz us a smoke, turf turk
just kick work shoot breeze
porter & sorter
sorting office raving adjacent
pre(o)positions // telegraphic conceits
naive [philandry] wild country
rescue me

virtuous quatrain / crypto
code, beautiful code, typifying
form, excelling sentiment
platform boots

cro lyrical entrapments

'contact / connection
gathering, assembly
public squares, loiter, linger,
non-abstract space
market space than a fast-paced
>   *commercial premises that*
>   *dominates* ~~*london's*~~ *[croydon's] streets*
sensory'

I

        pared down, little back roads,
dog and bull, spruced up, pukka fare.
        bilious, cr0 lyrical entrapments,
                the delta point, dark knight as
        croydon redress in gotham stylings.
up they rise, arbitrary modernists
                against rocking diatribe / death and
        deliverance, demanding the impossible,
a sick twisted hobgoblin splintering CPB territory —
                ruskin house on edge of folk and realism
        a nightmare weighing on the western brain.
                revolting conceptualism, the mind absorbed
in radiant shrill, burning fire for international modernisms,
                the calligraphic sweep of Shemza & co,
                Bowling's England, Aubrey's too
                the blissed out Baconian swelt
        skull life, lo' the (sub)urb is born,
my situationist recreation outta nowhere
                spurned for sedentary defraudment
NO FUTURE UTOPIA NOW
        at bottom of lyrical precis
                sold off on the stock exchange.
        louche and lucre
                lumpen fun, adventure for all,
herein lied plans for nowhere expanse
                NOWHERE

II

oral history
    under the word, over the top, even-keel
the words continue, my mind external,
    contiguous space, living space
I return to the fabled land — east croydon —
     workshopping down the portal orient — The Highway —
    space-time warped
turn to Narrow Street — in the Grapes — a
    shiply process — visible on the river —
return repeat, shapely jacket, DLR ventures, the
    can a tube moving trundle — play linguistic flail
— opportunity arise in graphic detail, the social-poetic release
    and the late PM moorings, returning to words,
visiting screen room / halls of wonder, what words
    do — paint and tune / my feeling iridescent
faux-discipline coursing out

              delete / live / organ's vehicle /
              a node / a non-place

III

running back in my own right

       my own peculiar way

cleaned it other day

       sedentary life

the big city dreams

       sound system pasts

georgian club, dingwall road

       modernists and subculturalists

the day will come

       old pretenders

new romantics, base antinomians

Acknowledgements

Previous versions of these poems have appeared in *MOTE, Zarf, Magma, Datableed, Paratext, Senna Hoy, BOOKS Review of Books, Tenebrae, algia, Lumin Journal, Ludd Gang, Site Projects, juf, Erotoplasty,* and *Tripwire,* the anthologies *We Want it All: An Anthology of Trans-Poetics* (Nightboat), *The Weird Folds (*Dostoevsky Wannabe*),* and *Responses to Love's Work (1995) by Gillian Rose* (Pilot Press) as well as the pamphlets *Relief I Willed it* (Gong Farm, 2021) and *fragments of mutability* (Earthbound, 2020), and the co-authored collection *Suburban Finesse* (Sad Press, 2021). Thanks to all the editors.

I must thank Azad for all the encouragement; to my mum and dad, Sangeeta and Ashwani, for setting this all up; and to Anuka for all the light.

LAY OUT YOUR UNREST

Milton Keynes UK
Ingram Content Group UK Ltd.
UKHW020822300524
443394UK00003B/135

9 781916 938113